Time Management

Stop Procrastinating

(Getting Things Done)

By

James Lewis

By applying the learnable time management skills in this book, readers will find more time for work, family, self-improvement or whatever is most important for them. The author provides you with a simple plan designed to improve your productivity and give you more time to do the things you want to do.

Dedication

To Sam, Chris, Patrick, Joshua, Jamie, Jessica and James Jr.

Without each one of you, I would have never perfected time management

Table of Contents

Chapter 1

Creating a List

"Begin somewhere."

-Liz Smith

THERE ARE TIMES WHEN we feel overwhelmed by the sheer amount of work that we have to complete. We are faced with numerous lists, targets, quotas and the likes. Moreover, we might be missing deadlines which can impact our professional lives. In other cases, we might tend to lose track of things, and tend to forget to do something critical. Alternatively we might try to save the task by finishing the job at the final hours. The symptoms mentioned here may be attributed to our inability in keeping a proper "to-do list". Creating a list is often the best way to ensure that prioritized tasks can be completed in an efficient and effective manner. A list can help you in completing the most important tasks, while keeping in mind that the least important tasks are to be prioritized later on.

Be organized.

A to-do list can help you to become organized and help keep track of things in a systematic way because all your tasks are written down in one place. This prevents you from forgetting the critical tasks that need to be immediately completed in a specific time frame. Being organized helps you to address the tasks that demand your immediate attention and your prompt work. This also helps in fighting work overload since it visually reminds you of the things that are yet to be accomplished. Aside from that, it can help to increase your focus and reliability because it helps you prioritize and be orderly. Being organized is an efficient way to combat stress because it gives you the knowledge and reassurance that you have listed everything and have not forgotten anything that are important to you, your career, your person life, your social life, and your other tasks at hand.

Learn the art of putting things into writing.

You must understand that you can never memorize all the tasks that you need to complete. You cannot simply trust your memory to keep track of all the numerous and various things and information that come your way every minute of every day. The limitations of trying to memorize important tasks become apparent once you forgot specific, and sometimes important, tasks. The best way to work through this is to put things into writing. Doing this simple thing can go a long way into letting you complete your work efficiently and effectively. It creates an avenue for you to have a single place where all the important tasks can be outlined and listed. In writing tasks, it is important to assign priority levels to each one. This will enormously help in letting you clearly see which ones need to be done as soon as possible and which ones can be put off to make way for much important tasks. It is also important to put the time and date of the deadline of each task so you can better estimated the time that you can allot to complete such tasks. It would also be helpful to note the time it takes for you to finish certain tasks. Writing tasks can be an important strategy in fighting procrastination as it can provide to be a clear and visual reminder of the things that are yet to be accomplished.

Prepare your schedule each night.

Preparing for tomorrow is the key element of having a list. A list helps you to prepare for the future in a reliable and flexible manner. By planning the following day that you will be having, you are able to have a schedule which must be adhered to in order to complete all the tasks. It would help you visualize how your day will go so that you will have a certain expectation for each day, as well as a planned outcome after each day. The schedule should be flexible enough to add time for tasks that can arise unexpectedly and deviate from your schedule. Distractions also need to be taken into account when creating schedules in an efficient and effective manner. This way, you can have buffer or safeguard timeslots that are intended for you to overcome surprise tasks and unexpected delays.

Prioritize your tasks.

Once you have written your tasks, it is important to assign priorities ranging from A (very critical) to F (least important). Assigning priorities will help you to become comfortable with the great amount of tasks that you are faced with. Through this, you will be able to learn the ability to manage time in a proper and efficient manner. You have to remember to always check your list when you have many tasks that have a high priority. Creating different types of lists is also helpful, especially in cases where you may have many tasks with high priority. This will help you be more organized and detail-oriented to certain immediate tasks that you are focusing on at the moment. However you must also remember to make your to-do lists simple in a way that it should avoid confusion. The best strategy is to use a combination of different lists as a means of ensuring efficiency.

Chapter 2

Knowing Your Wants and Needs

"A mind troubled by doubt cannot focus on the course to victory."

-Arthur Golden

SELF-REFLECTION IS THE KEY to combating stress and procrastination. It is important that you come up with specific and measurable objectives. You have to know which ones are your needs and which ones are your wants. You have to differentiate which ones are vital in your day-to-day life and which ones you can survive without at the meantime. Aside from this, you must also strive to create a specific routine that can help you in completing the immediate needed tasks. All of these strategies must be used in coordination with each other in order to produce superior outcomes.

Take time to reflect.

Self-reflection is very important when pursuing a time management strategy. This is because it is a very helpful way through which you can examine and assess your work as well as your routine. You can frequently assess the relevance, the efficiency, and the performance of your specific tasks and activities. This is also an opportunity for you to reflect upon the impact of certain activities to your personal goals and objectives. Spending some time to engage in self-reflection will certainly help you to obtain an idea about your key strengths and weaknesses, your immediate needs and regular wants, your priorities and other concerns. Moreover, you will also be able to create a superior strategy for success through this step of motivation, prioritization, and reflection.

Learn to say no.

Oftentimes, we are overwhelmed with tasks because we simply refuse to say "no". We do this out of a misguided notion of feeling guilt, of having inner conflicts, or even trying to act like we can perform all the work activities all at once. This can be avoided by humbly knowing your limits and respectfully using the simple word "no". One way to do this is to use a sympathetic but assertive tone. You can explain your reason, the amount of workload you have at the moment and the amount of time you have left to allot or even the scarce amount of time that you may have rest. Refusing tasks will help you from being overwhelmed or overstressed, but you have to remember to still be respectful and polite about it. You have to keep in mind that walking away or changing the subject may have the desired effect of you dodging some work, but remember that this can backfire and leave the person you're talking to with a sense that you are irresponsible or lazy. There are other effective ways of refusing to do certain tasks to avoid being overworked and overstressed. You can complete your current schedule in an effectual manner without you having to step on others.

Eliminate the non-essential.

Do not allow unimportant details to drag you down. Many people get frustrated because they are unable to eliminate the trivial details in their work. Focusing and stressing on not-so-important matters can certainly reduce productivity and output. You have to know that some minor tasks can be done in a simple and efficient alternative ways that can take up a lot less time that it would do for certain major tasks. It is important to identify the minor details in your to-do list in order for you to have the time to concentrate on the important tasks at hand. Such an approach will really be beneficial to individuals because it can create strong focus, adequate attention, and necessary concentration to be given on the immediate tasks that need to be completed.

Eliminate distractions.

There are many types of distractions that exist which can reduce your ability to focus on important tasks. Eliminating distractions is one of the key strategies in combating procrastination. Having proper focus is important in all kinds of tasks. Appropriate focus can be effectively established by having motivating messages and reminders that can help you to further concentrate on the key tasks. Remind yourself of the importance of the tasks so that you remain involved and motivated. It also important to take a break once in a while when you start to feel fatigue and when distractions become too problematic. There's

11

nothing wrong with taking a break. This can even have the chance to reboot your focus, energy and strength after you decide to take a stroll, listen to music, watch a clip, entertain yourself with an article or a post online, or even just close your eyes for several minutes. These can certainly help in regaining back your focus and attention.

Establish routines.

Most people learn that following a daily task or routine can help them go through their day-to-day activities. A proper routine can help you to complete the tasks in a reliable manner. Working intelligently is the solution to many problems and challenges. This can be done by knowing your capabilities and attention span, and also by giving you time to adjust to certain tasks. Having a fixed routine can be beneficial because you have the focus to complete the daily tasks before trying to move on to complete other work.

Chapter 3

Setting-up a Goal

"Dreams are extremely important. You can't do it unless you imagine it."

-George Lucas

GOAL-SETTING IS A POWERFUL endeavor which helps you to have a clear vision about the future. Aside from that, it can also motivate you in transforming your dreams into realities. It is an important part of time management because through this, you can plan your steps and choose where you want to go in life. Goal-setting helps you to have the proper knowledge and preparations needed regarding your future. With this, you can concentrate on the activities that are in accordance with your goals. This can also help you identify distractions and challenges that are likely to prevent or hinder you from achieving your maximum potential, and consequently, your success in reaching your dreams.

Set-up goals.

Goals should be established at multiple levels in order to achieve success. It is important that you start with the life goals which help you to give an idea about what you want to do with your life. The large scale goals need to be identified at this stage.

14

After that, you can break the goals into smaller and smaller targets. Once these goals have been identified then you can develop a comprehensive strategy to accomplish them. Work activities can be divided into smaller tasks which can be easily completed. Having goals helps you to attain a clear idea about the future.

Set-up time limits.

Parkinson's Law states that the more time is given to complete a certain task, the complexity of this task increases. Some tasks can become daunting as you witness an increase in tension and stress. The best strategy to overcome this is to establish time limits on specific tasks. Having an understanding about the approximate time that it will take you to complete tasks is certainly an efficient way of managing time. Knowing the right amount of time for tasks can help you to gain more time for other tasks. Through this, you can better plan and you can better prepare which of your hours will be spent on a certain task, and which will be allotted to another.

15

Do it!

Put into actions what your plans and goals for the day are. Establishing goals is a futile endeavor if you do not implement strategies to accomplish key targets. Taking appropriate action that your plans need in order to be implemented can be taken as a means of helping to boost your confidence and motivation to complete tasks. All the plans must be realistic and viable in order to avoid the chances of failure. You have to know which ones are the necessary steps that simply cannot be skipped, and which ones can be simplified or incorporated into other important steps. With this strategy, you can better prepare your mind and your body to have the confidence and self-assurance that you need before you have to actually do the actions.

Don't waste your goals.

Goal setting should be done in a systematic and methodical manner. You must have a clear understanding about the different processes and strategies that are needed to accomplish your targets. You should not let any one of your goals be put to waste. Once you've set it as one of your goals, you should prepare well for it and work with passion and diligence. With hard work and patience comes success. You will soon see understand reaping what you sown.

Implement your actions well.

Goals should be realistic and viable in order to ensure success within a practical period of time. Implementing the strategies to complete goals is one of the crucial parts of time management. It is important to review and audit the strategies so that the chances of success can be increased within a short period of time. You should assess your plans well, as well as strategize ahead what choices and actions you expect to encounter in order to reach your goals. You need to be better prepared to face them when the need arises, and in doing so, you will also lessen being sidetracked by surprises and unexpected things that could have been prevented in the first place.

Chapter 4

Working Smart

"Do not be too timid and squeamish about your actions. All life is an experiment."

-Ralph Waldo Emerson

THE HECTIC LIFESTYLE AND increasing workload that are common to everyone reaching for success means that you need to work smartly. Such a feat is possible if you will use proper time management strategies. Increasing efficiency as well as enhancing productivity are some of the ways that you can work smartly. You must always focus on eliminating distractions in order to improve your quality of work. Taking small breaks is also beneficial because it helps you to enhance your productivity. Aside from that, it is also really helpful to know how to delegate your workload properly in order to increase productivity and at the same time avoid being overstressed and overworked.

Quality.

It is important to give focus on the quality of work accomplished. One way to do this is to identify the time periods when you can work at optimum levels. You should know yourself enough to know the kind of environment that you will work best in. You should further develop strategies that will help you

20

to improve your quality of work. You can also try to find ways to increase productivity and output. Whether it be in a busy and active environment or a quiet and serene one, you should know which of these will best help you in producing quality work. Through this, you will know to avoid the time and space where none of your comfortable workplace is present. This will also help you avoid distractions, such as lengthy conversations during breaks, social media websites, attending unnecessary meetings, distractions that will most likely affect how you produce and accomplish excellent and quality pieces of work.

Quantity.

The quantity of work you produce is also an important focus. The quantity of work that you accomplish should always be based upon realistic goals. You should know your strengths and limitations so that you can avoid agreeing to certain tasks that are more than the ones you can actually accomplish. You should not let yourself reach your breaking point by taking on more tasks than you should. This will not only affect the quantity and quality of the work you accomplish, but it will also greatly affect your health. You should avoid overstressing and overworking yourself by breaking larger and complex tasks into smaller ones. Such a strategy will certainly help you to gradually and surely complete your complex and numerous amount of work.

Check your time.

Using time efficiently is one of the key aspects of working smartly. Distractions can range from small and trivial ones to large and potentially damaging ones. You should always try to have a realistic strategy that can be used to combat distractions in a proficient manner. One way to do is to always be conscious of the amount of time that you allot into a certain task. You should avoid lingering too much on one task that can actually be accomplished in such a short and quick time. Tasks such as answering emails, responding to inquiries, and taking phone calls should not take so much of your time as making presentations, working on spreadsheets, or drafting letters.

Take a break.

Learn to take a break when you feel that you will overwhelm yourself. Short breaks between work activities certainly help in rejuvenating your minds. You will also be able to successfully rethink about the tasks you're working on if ever you are faced with difficulties. Short breaks tend to relax the mind, as well as give you the opportunity to move away from the work environment for a moment. Taking a brisk walk, closing your eyes, or drinking water and eating snacks will help in refreshing your mind, your body, and your energy to continue on with your work at hand. It also helps to eat healthy snacks like fruits or vegetables as they can help relax and nourish your body. Aside from that, it is also helpful to talk to someone who you enjoy being with to break the fatigue and stress you may start to feel with your immense workload after a certain time.

Outsource.

Although it is important to have the confidence and self-assurance to finish your tasks, you must also understand that you cannot complete all the work activities simply on your own. It certainly wouldn't hurt to seek the help of others, especially with tasks that may either require the knowledge of an expert or simply the support of other people to help carry on the load. It is important to delegate some tasks to your juniors if possible, or merely to assign to another person to look over certain tasks that will be better done with their assistance. Delegation helps you to focus on your core competencies. With this, you are also able to successfully improve your concentration and attention towards the immediate important tasks. Additionally, this approach will also help you to not only save time, but also to avoid stress and anxiety that you may acquire from your immense workload.

Chapter 5

Meeting Your Goals

"The future depends on what you do today."

-Mahatma Gandhi

MEETING THE GOALS THAT you have set for yourself is a crucial aspect of time management. These goals are important for your life success, as well as the means to attain your dreams. You have to learn to perform your tasks in an efficient manner while focusing on promptness and excellence. To meet your goals, you need to have a strong desire to achieve them. You have to have the will and determination to go through with the necessary actions needed to achieve your dreams. You have to continuously keep this in mind as weak resolve and willpower more often produce weak results. Having a strong resolution and a resilient drive will certainly go a long way into helping you meet your goals.

Be on time.

Promptness is the key to completing all the goals that you have created. This is because of the fact that being prompt will help you to be active and well-prepared for any unforeseeable circumstances. Being on time, or sometimes even being ahead of schedule, helps in giving a leeway or buffer period for you to still perform and accomplish other unexpected tasks that may arise. Aside from this, you can spend time to plan major goals that you need to accomplish. Promptness will certainly pay-off because you can quickly move on to the next tasks, while also having the feeling of a sense of accomplishment when you have completed one of your goals. Promptness will indeed help you in ensuring a smooth functioning of your job, as well as preventing imminent inconveniences that might be encountered in the work environment.

Do your best.

Always show excellence in all aspects of tasks that you accomplish in order to complete your work activities efficiently and excellently. Bad habits in your work environment will not only slow your career, but also increase stress that can affect your work, social, and personal life. They can also create negative circumstances which might jeopardize your work activities. Doing your best ultimately helps you to complete the job activities in an efficient manner. Moreover, you are able to further develop and monitor your progress as you will continuously strive to acquire successful habits. Through this, you can improve and better visualize your future self as you complete your goals. Having good work ethics and a picture of your improved self can be a good strategy in meeting the objectives that can consequently lead to your success.

What done is done.

Once you have completed the task, do not waste time on it. This is important to remember because not doing so will only cause a loss in productivity and efficiency. It will create unnecessary distractions which will prevent you from moving to the next level. However, it is important to check that the goal has been completed in a perfect manner. Being critical and particular of your actions and choices along your journey to success will help you to describe the major accomplishments along the way. These key steps can help you to transform your goals into reality.

Move forward.

It is important to understand that all goals are created at different levels, the first of which is the blueprint which will help you towards the path to success. It helps to give you an idea about what you desire and what you wish to accomplish. The second level is the action plan which will then transform your goals into reality. This shows the levels of appropriate steps needed that you have to move forward to so that you can continue towards the path of success. Various goals will be evaluated at certain levels, which mean that you must continue to use a realistic strategy for you to reach the top of the ladder towards success.

Chapter 6

Stepping Back

"A decision is only as strong as the belief standing behind it."

-Isaiah Hankel

DECISION MAKING SHOULD BE conducted in a proper manner as ad hoc decisions might jeopardize your time management strategies and eventually, your long term goals. The best way to avoid this kind of problems is to have a comprehensive strategy for responding to problems. Many activities that we engage in do not bring benefit with respect to us, and to our life goals. Furthermore, we waste precious resources, time, and energy on these inconsequential activities. The 80/20 rule is an important strategy in fighting procrastination. This strategy can help in achieving the desired results in life provided you have identified the things that are most important for you, which typically make up only 20% of your tasks. Aside from that, thinking out of the box is a creative means to solve problems. Since time management is also about being able to resolve your problems in an efficient manner, thinking of new and innovative ways to deal with problems and challenges will help you to achieve your life goals within a short period of time.

Take time before making decisions.

Decision making is important part of time management that's why you have to allot the time and effort that is necessary to make proper decisions. You need to be careful so as not to make quick, hasty, irrational, and impractical decisions. This is because decisions such as these will often result in the inability to achieve goals. This may be a cause of you being unable to successfully focus on the core activities that can bring you success. Just take some time so that you can reflect on the advantages and disadvantages of certain action plans and strategies. You have to know which of these steps or goals you really want and really need. Having a comprehensive idea about the entire process and the whole impact of things can certainly help you in making big decisions which will soon have a huge effect on your life. Decision making is a process that should be undertaken in a smart, rational, and sensible manner.

80/20 Pareto Principle

The Pareto Principle can prove to be an important strategy in time management because it states that only a few, typically making up 20% of your total tasks, are truly important, while the majority, typically making up 80% of the total, can actually be considered unimportant. This principle helps you to understand that you must give your focus and attention to the 20%, since it is deemed to have the most importance in your life. You need to focus on the 20% through proper planning and preparation. There will come a time in your life where you will encounter lots of resources-consuming and time-wasting activities. This can be troublesome as it can lead to negative implications. This is another problem that can be alleviated by the Pareto Principle, because once you discover the important and unimportant things in your life, you will be able to achieve better productivity and output.

Think out of the box.

Thinking out of the box is very important, especially in dealing with tasks that are time-dependent. We are often faced with difficult and challenging tasks in life that hinder our improvement and development. The best way to deal with this is to brainstorm about different ideas which has the potential to help not only open up the thinking processes, but also eventually aid in solving challenges that we are stuck with. Brainstorming helps you to find creative solutions for your problems. There are numerous problems that are very perplexing and challenging, most of which require creative solutions. This means that thinking out of the box can certainly help you in overcoming them. The individual must be able to use circumstances, capacity, capability, and vision in order to overcome these difficulties. Aside from that, thinking of new ways to provide solutions to tasks will help you deal with your limitations, thereby lessening the circumstances where you will exhaust yourself and consume all your resources.

Chapter 7

Taking Care of Yourself

"Work to become, not to acquire."

-Elbert Hubbard

ONE OF THE IMPORTANT things that must never be neglected is your health. You must take care of yourself through proper exercise, healthy eating, and proper sleep. Exercise helps to rejuvenate your body and your mind. This will really help in ensuring the highest levels of productivity and success within a considerable period of time. Aside from exercise, it also helps to create a superior strategy that can be used to attain success in the long term. Proper eating ensures that you are healthy enough to meet deadlines, deal with tasks, and manage time in an efficient and effective manner. You should never deprive yourself of sleep, as this will have both short-term and long-term effects such as inability to focus, loss of concentration and energy, or even heart problems. Socializing with others is also seen as an important activity for a person's health because it helps you to relax and release your stress. Through this, you can share problems with others, while you also enjoy the time by relaxing and giving yourself a well-needed break.

Have a healthy diet.

Healthy eating can help you to release stress, as well as to concentrate on the important tasks that need to be completed. Avoid eating fried or greasy food, and also processed foods. Natural vegetables and fruits are excellent for maintaining body health and strength. Healthy eating also protects you from mental and physical fatigue. A healthy mind and body can help you to manage your time properly, as well as to keep yourself in a continuous state of alert and energy. Procrastination and laziness can be combated through healthy eating as it can help give strength, and also help guide your body and mind in the proper direction to accomplish the given tasks at hand.

Give importance to proper exercise.

Proper exercise is a great way to relax the body, which can have an effect on your focus and concentration on more important things. Time management is about having adequate energy which can be used by the body for performing complex sets of tasks. Exercise helps to keep you in a state of fitness so that you can resist physical and mental fatigue. Like a healthy diet, proper exercise can also be a comforting and relaxing activity which will help you to remain in a healthy and strong state. Exercise should be done in accordance with your requirements and capabilities, something that is appropriate to your abilities and endurance.

Get adequate sleep.

Sleep is considered a vital factor for you when you want to combat stress and anxiety. Adequate sleep means having at least 6 hours of sleep every night. Sleep helps to heal your body and mind, while it filters out the key stressors in your life. Along with proper exercise and eating, having enough sleep can certainly help enhance your energy levels. Because of this, you will then be able to perform efficiently in the work environment. Proper sleep helps restore the vitality and strength of the body. You can wake up fresh in the morning with the ability to perform your tasks excellently.

Socialize with others.

Socializing is an important activity that should also not be disregarded for its seemingly trivial and small effects. Through this, your state of being is generally improved because you get to share and exchange information with different people, and you also have the chance to take a break and relax at the same time. You can meet people who have similar interests as you, which can really prove to be a relaxing and stimulating activity for you. Meeting up with friends means that you are able to share important details of your life and theirs. This will not only create a stress-free environment, but it can also lead to sound outcomes and products within a short period of time.

Chapter 8

Knowing Yourself

"You'll never know what you're capable of if you don't try."

-Sheryl Sandberg

IT IS IMPORTANT THAT you know your key strengths, weaknesses, limitations, and capabilities. You must complete a comprehensive analysis of yourself so that you can understand yourself, your personality, and your abilities better. Through this, you will have the chance to develop a strategic plan of action for your success. Aside from that, knowing your capabilities and limitations will help you work on your weaknesses, while also develop ways for you to further build and improve your strengths. This will also help you in assessing the amount of work you can handle so that you can accept only those that you are able to complete. It is through the use of innovative and creative approaches that success can be attained.

Know your strengths and capabilities.

It is important to have knowledge of your major competencies, talents, expertise, skills, and habits. This will help you to become positive and motivated in completing activities. Furthermore, you will be able to focus on building your strengths as a means of improvement. Self-development is concerned with raising the consciousness and awareness of human beings. In a work environment, it helps to further increase the productivity and competence of the workforce so as to improve the quality of work produced. It can crate efficient work processes, as well as reduce wasted effort. Continuous learning is beneficial because it helps in improving career opportunities and also providing incentives that ensure personal growth. Finally, self-development leads to high levels of improvement in various aspects such as technical, personal, and managerial skills.

Know your weaknesses.

A realistic knowledge about weaknesses is important because through this, you can devise strategies to overcome them. Viable and robust strategies can be employed as a means of overcoming weaknesses within a short period of time. Personal self-knowledge is also critical for success because it helps you to enhance your abilities and competencies. Having the chance to develop yourself is really beneficial to both yourself and your career; it can give you a sense of satisfaction and achievement. Furthermore, self-knowledge can be essential for resolving complex business situations. With this, you are given the opportunity to work on your qualities that need improvement. Aside from that, appropriate approaches towards self-knowledge can also increase the chances of promotions and incentives for you since you can show others including your fellows and possibly your employers, how much you have learned and acquired.

Have patience.

Patience is a very important part of time management for various reasons. Firstly, patience helps you to understand your goals. Secondly, patience will be able to help you devise effective and realistic goals. Finally, you will be able to work slowly so that you can meet the goals. Taking the time to actually learn and appreciate the advantages and disadvantages can certainly help in your better understanding of your life missions. Aside from that, you will also be able to devise viable and realistic strategies for change. With patience, you are given the ability to deal with problems in an efficient and appropriate manner.

Know your limitations.

Nobody is perfect. Always know your limitations. It is good to aim for perfection in everything that you do, but it is also important to keep in mind that no one is perfect. Having the inability to understand this important thought can have the effect of often having trouble in deriving satisfaction from work activities that have been completed. You have to remember to adapt a realistic yet positive attitude when you have completed your tasks and activities. Such an approach will help you to appreciate the strengths and weaknesses of your moves. If problems arise, at least you know that you can complete your work next time with better results since you will know you have learned your mistakes.

44

Aside from that, understanding your limitations can help you in being assertive yet respectful when you know you are unable be finish more tasks, as well as in letting yourself refuse tasks without feeling incompetent and useless. In actuality, you have actually done the proper thing of being honest, practical, and rational by knowing your capabilities and your limitations.

Chapter 9

Rewarding Yourself and Others

"Communication - the human connection - is the key to personal and career success."

-Paul J. Meyer

SELF-REWARD IS AN important part of time management because it helps you to gain a sense of satisfaction and fulfillment. It also helps you to concentrate on the tasks which can eventually help you to become highly successful in life. Aside from that, you have to remember to give credit and recognition to those people who have been part of the process and journey to motivate and push you to where you are now.

Praise yourself for a job well-done.

Praise is an important part of rewarding yourself once you have completed a critical task. Praise is a motivator. It gives a sense of achievement which can be used to attain efficiency and effectiveness in future work. Praise helps to create increased levels of confidence and attainment among individuals. Satisfaction gives you the self-assurance that you have the ability to face future challenges, as well as the strength to deal with and overcome other problems.

Give yourself something.

Reward yourself when you have completed a critical task. This may be in the form of various things such as going out to your favorite restaurant, watching your favorite movie, hanging out with friends, or buying yourself something new. It could also involve traveling to some tourist destination and giving yourself a well-needed break. It can even be a simple reward like reading a book, or spending a peaceful day at home. It can actually range to a million other things, but the basic premise is that you should reward yourself for accomplishing feats, and give yourself a break and a sense of fulfillment for all that you have achieved.

Give credits.

One of the most important things to remember along your journey to success is that you should never forget those that helped you to get where you are. The best way to show your thanks and sincerity to these people is by giving them credit as someone who has supported you in completing your endeavors and pushing past your challenges. This will certainly help you in creating a congenial work environment, which can certainly lead to long term success within a short period of time. You should be grateful to others for the help they have given. Never forget them when you reach success. You have to remember that all their opinions, advice and support were great contributions in you achieving and attaining your goals and your success.

www.ingramcontent.com/pod-product-compliance
Lightning Source LLC
Chambersburg PA
CBHW051246170526
45165CB00004B/1600